Read Super Fast

What you need to start (and stop) doing to increase reading speed and comprehension.

www.readsuperfast.com

Introduction

There's a lot to be said about reading for pleasure. Few things are more luxurious than reveling in metaphors or dawdling over particularly brilliant passages – the kind you return to over and over again for the sheer enjoyment of it.

Reading for business or study purposes, however, is a completely different matter. It's quick and dirty, transactional and mercenary. The aim is to dive in, extract what you need and parachute out. This kind of reading is geared towards ruthlessly maximizing ROI (Return on Investment) – putting in the least amount of time and effort in order to achieve the highest possible return.

The kinds of texts you'll read during your professional life will be manuals, journal articles, case studies, textbooks and the like, but even blog posts, RSS feeds and nonfiction books. To get the most out of them, you'll need to adopt an entirely new style of reading far removed from the way you might tackle a novel.

Imagine how much material you could get through if you could double or triple your reading speed. You might think that speed readers don't really understand what they're reading, but comprehension and speed are not mutually exclusive. It's all about technique. And speed reading is about working smarter, not harder.

Reading is one of the main ways we absorb information, and learning to read more efficiently will enable you to take in and retain more knowledge without belaboring the process. Effective speed reading involves reading with a clear end purpose in mind so that you only read relevant material, and employing other strategies to streamline your reading process.

The first step is to **decide** you are going to increase your reading speed, and **trust** that you can do it. It obviously is the case since you're holding this book in your hands. But it is also an extremely important factor. **Commit** to increasing your speed and comprehension, have that as your goal every time you read from now on, and by integrating your commitment with the techniques described here, you'll be doubling or tripling your reading speed in no time.

Habits you need to break

Learning to speed read won't happen overnight. In a sense, you are almost relearning how to read, retraining your eyes and brain to operate in a different manner. You learned to read when you were a child, but then stopped developing that ability. Most people today still read at the speed of a 12 year old. Here are some common habits you've probably developed over the years that you'll need to overcome in order to increase your reading speed.

Vocalizing

You're probably sounding out words unconsciously as you read, a throwback to your school days when reading out loud was how you learned. Vocalizing, however, limits how fast you can read. If you're saying every word aloud in you head, you are restricting your reading speed to your talking speed. (You might even mutter the words silently to yourself.) And as anyone can tell you, we can read a lot faster than we can physically speak.

In fact, your reading abilities, on the other hand, are more on par with your thinking speed. No matter how fast you talk, you can't enunciate more than a single word at a time. We can speak aloud at a rate of about 200 words a minute, but we are capable of reading – and thinking – **many** times faster than that. Think about that, how many things can you think about simultaneously? Just a few seconds of thought could yield dozens, or even hundreds of pages of content if you were able to put everything into words.

Need to kick the vocalization habit? There's nothing for it but practice. Try reading faster than you normally would. If the voice in your head fails to keep up and fades away, you're on the right track. You can also try counting 1, 2, 3, 4 rhythmically as you read to get you into a faster groove. Placing a pen or similar object between your lips will quickly let you know if you've fallen back into mouthing the words. Another useful technique is to "hum" as you read (even out loud), so that you can "cover up" the words you would otherwise be reading out loud.

Remember: **reading isn't just about seeing words on a page; it's about absorbing ideas and synthesizing information.**

Backtracking

It's natural to go back and read over sentences that you didn't quite grasp the first time around, even though you just read it. Also bear in mind that your eyes generally don't stay focused on one spot continuously. Rather, they flicker around – and every movement requires a readjustment, costing you precious time. Your eyes are capable of moving very quickly, but the slower you go, the more likely they are to wander.

The bad news: this "one step forward, two steps back" habit will seriously slow you down. Resist the urge to re-read material you think you might have missed, and carry on. Trust that you have the ability to understand what you're reading, and that you have more than one opportunity to find the meaning ahead. Books tend to expand on points over the course of entire paragraphs, so you'll have plenty more opportunity to absorb the message if you simply continue reading. Press on forward!

One way to train your eyes to read smoothly in one direction is to use your hand as a guide. Move your hand gradually down the page, keeping your finger pointed at the line you are currently reading. Maintain a consistent and brisk speed. Or you could do this with a piece of paper or cardboard. Just slide it down the page as you read, blocking out parts you've already read and keeping your eyes focused on the next lines. Another alternative is to use your index finger or a pen, so your eyes follow that movement – this will also help reduce eye strain.

Reading every single word

This is perhaps the most important lesson, and represents a step up from the others. Growing up, you were probably taught to read word by word or letter by letter, sounding out syllables. But with practice, you can learn to read blocks of words (and there are some words, like 'the' or 'an', that can be skipped entirely – they don't add anything to a text, so you won't miss them). With this technique, The PX Project, a three-hour cognitive experiment at Princeton University, claimed an average increase in reading speed of 386% among participants.

Learning how to use your peripheral vision is key to successful speed reading. You don't need to read every single word in its own right. Your eyes and brain are both capable of taking in many words at once. This is known as 'chunking' – or reading multiple words at the same time.

Chunking is the driving format behind telephone numbers, credit card numbers, and the like. It's common knowledge that humans do better when recalling numbers in groups, rather than one long unbroken string.

You'll need to learn to relax your gaze while reading, opening up your peripheral vision in order to see groups of words rather than individual words.

Try this practice exercise: focus on a central strip of vertical text down the middle of a page. Keep your eyes directed on this column, but try to indirectly take in the words to each side of this area as well. Imagine that your eyes are sponges, and you need to soak up all you possibly can while keeping them firmly trained in the middle. You should still be able to perceive the words towards the edges of the page at the same time. Holding the page farther away from your eyes can help. It's also worth doing this exercise with a newspaper, practicing reading line by line (rather than word by word) down the narrow columns on each page.

elevator	←→	blue
nice elevator	←→	blue antique
very nice elevator	←→	blue antique car
slow very nice elevator	←→	vintage blue antique car

Once you've gotten used to that, try dividing up a page into three equal vertical columns. Try to see all of the words in a sentence within that 'third' of the page. Practice this until you become accustomed to this 'expanded' gaze.

Thanks to peripheral vision, you don't actually need to read every word in every sentence. Skipping the first and last 2-3 words in every line will still enable you to absorb the information (sort of an inverse of the way humans can generally understand scrambled words, as long as the first and last letters remain the same). Your eyes will still take in those introductory and ending words without going to the effort of focusing directly on them. This method is known as 'indenting'.

To train yourself, we'll go back to the technique we used to break the habit of backtracking. Use your finger – or a pen (which provides a sharper focal point) – to track along under each sentence as you read it. Start a few towards in from the left margin, and stop a few words before reaching the end of a sentence. Don't let your eyes drift towards those beginnings and endings. Learning to 'see' to the sides dramatically reduces the effort your brain and eyes need to expend during the course of reading a text.

Top-heavy

Your brain is a lot sharper than you might give it credit for, and you might be surprised to learn that we can easily recognize letters just by seeing the top half of each character. Make the most of this opportunity to speed up your reading even further. Focus only on the upper parts of each printed sentence and see how much of a difference that makes.

The Z method

Reading Western style is fairly linear. Left to right, top to bottom. But while it might *feel* as if you're reading in a straight line, your eyes are in fact moving in imperceptible fits and jumps. Each phrase ends with a brief fixation (a snapshot, almost) on an area of text within your peripheral vision.

What does this mean for a would-be speed reader? Well, the brain is an amazing organ; it's constantly working overtime trying to make sense of all the information it's processing, filling in the blanks where it can and reconciling new information with prior knowledge. This means that not only are you capable of moving beyond a word-by-word reading paradigm, you don't even have to restrict yourself to reading line by line.

The Z method revolves around reading along a zigzag pattern. First, you read a single line normally. Secondly, once you reach the end of the sentence, you sweep your eyes from right to left across the next line in a diagonal motion, landing on the beginning of the third sentence. Rinse and repeat all the way down a page.

Advanced techniques

A key tenet of speed reading is that you don't need to read it all from beginning to end. That's not cheating; it's simply a way of working more efficiently. Here are some more tips to help you along the way.

Indenting

We've already established that it's important to break the habit of painstakingly reading word by word, because the number of words you read increases your reading speed.

Thanks to peripheral vision, you don't actually need to read every word in every sentence. Skipping the first and last 2-3 words in every line will still enable you to absorb the information (sort of an inverse of the way humans can generally understand scrambled words, as long as the first and last letters remain the same). Your eyes will still take in those introductory and ending words without going to the effort of focusing directly on them. This method is known as 'indenting'.

To train yourself, we'll go back to the technique we used to break the habit of backtracking. Use your finger – or a pen (which provides a sharper focal point) – to track along under each sentence as you read it. Start a few towards in from the left margin, and stop a few words before reaching the end of a sentence. Don't let your eyes drift towards those beginnings and endings. Learning to 'see' to the sides dramatically reduces the effort your brain and eyes need to expend during the course of reading a text.

Top-heavy

Your brain is a lot sharper than you might give it credit for, and you might be surprised to learn that we can easily recognize letters just by seeing the top half of each character. Make the most of this opportunity to speed up your reading even further. Focus only on the upper parts of each printed sentence and see how much of a difference that makes.

The Z method

Reading Western style is fairly linear. Left to right, top to bottom. But while it might *feel* as if you're reading in a straight line, your eyes are in fact moving in imperceptible fits and jumps. Each phrase ends with a brief fixation (a snapshot, almost) on an area of text within your peripheral vision.

What does this mean for a would-be speed reader? Well, the brain is an amazing organ; it's constantly working overtime trying to make sense of all the information it's processing, filling in the blanks where it can and reconciling new information with prior knowledge. This means that not only are you capable of moving beyond a word-by-word reading paradigm, you don't even have to restrict yourself to reading line by line.

The Z method revolves around reading along a zigzag pattern. First, you read a single line normally. Secondly, once you reach the end of the sentence, you sweep your eyes from right to left across the next line in a diagonal motion, landing on the beginning of the third sentence. Then repeat all the way down a page.

As you learn to 'see' more on the page, you'll no longer need to focus on every line. While you might think this would lead to you missing vital information, your eyes and brain can in fact pick up and process those zigzagged lines without too much trouble. With practice, you could even expand this to a six-line Z, sweeping diagonally across two lines every time instead of just one.

Thanks to peripheral vision, you don't actually need to read every word in every sentence. Skipping the first and last 2-3 words in every line will still enable you to absorb the information (sort of an inverse of the way humans can generally understand scrambled words, as long as the first and last letters remain the same). Your eyes will still take in those introductory and ending words without going to the effort of focusing directly on them. This method is known as 'indenting'.

To train yourself, we'll go back to the technique we used to break the habit of backtracking. Use your finger – or a pen (which provides a sharper focal point) – to track along under each sentence as you read it. Start a few towards in from the left margin, and stop a few words before reaching the end of a sentence. Don't let your eyes drift towards those beginnings and endings. Learning to 'see' to the sides dramatically reduces the effort your brain and eyes need to expend during the course of reading a text.

Top-heavy

Your brain is a lot sharper than you might give it credit for, and you might be surprised to learn that we can easily recognize letters just by seeing the top half of each character. Make the most of this opportunity to speed up your reading even further. Focus only on the upper parts of each printed sentence and see how much of a difference that makes.

The Z method

Reading Western style is fairly linear. Left to right, top to bottom. But while it might *feel* as if you're reading in a straight line, your eyes are in fact moving in imperceptible fits and jumps. Each phrase ends with a brief fixation (a snapshot, almost) on an area of text within your peripheral vision.

What does this mean for a would-be speed reader? Well, the brain is an amazing organ; it's constantly working overtime trying to make sense of all the information it's processing, filling in the blanks where it can and reconciling new information with prior knowledge. This means that not only are you capable of moving beyond a word-by-word reading paradigm, you don't even have to restrict yourself to reading line by line.

The Z method revolves around reading along a zigzag pattern. First, you read a single line normally. Secondly, once you reach the end of the sentence, you sweep your eyes from right to left across the next line in a diagonal motion, landing on the beginning of the third sentence. Rinse and repeat all the way down a page.

If the Z method works well for you, try rounding those sharp corners into a smoother curve – more of an S than a Z – and weave down the page in a more relaxed pattern. The more fluid your visual path, the faster you can go.

Mixing up your speed

Not all words in any given piece of reading material are made equal. Likewise, you don't need to give every one an equal amount of your attention.

You may want to slow down to take in points that are emphasized in bold or italics or to concentrate on a passage that's bogged down in technical jargon.

Another good rule of thumb is to slow down for the first sentence in a paragraph; these usually contain the main idea, which is why they're known as topic sentences. The following sentences generally provide further evidence to support this point, and may not warrant as much time. Content that treads familiar ground can be skimmed over, giving you more time to spend on absorbing new material.

Key takeaway

Speed reading strategies all center around one unifying theme: creating a smoother 'flow' as you read, and shifting the focus from single words to larger blocks – phrases, sentences, paragraphs. This enables you to quickly grasp the key messages and concepts in a passage – seeing the forest rather than just the trees. Try to dismiss the notion that you need to 'see' everything on a page in order to take it in, or that you must read every single word from beginning to end. Once you're comfortable with the notion that you don't need to painstakingly work your way through every sentence, paragraph, and chapter, you can progress much faster and step away as soon as you've absorbed all you need to know.

Practice makes permanent

There's only one way to increase your reading speed, and that's practice. But this means focused practice with the right techniques. They say practice makes perfect, but if you practice a wrong technique recurringly, you will just guarantee to have the poor technique ingrained permanently! So indeed practice makes permanent. And to ensure your end result is perfect, you need to make sure you are practicing the correct techniques as described in this book.

If you want to read faster, time yourself (use a stopwatch, or use one of the many reading speed testing tools online). You'll then have a starting point from which you can improve.

As with developing any new habit, consistency is crucial. Keep plugging away and drilling techniques until they become second nature. Giving up early on will only set you back.

Measuring improvement

You can't improve what you don't measure. If you're serious about learning to speed read, testing yourself is the only way to gauge whether you're getting faster – the numbers don't lie.

Calculating your reading speed is a fairly straightforward undertaking, obtained by taking the number of words you read and dividing it by the amount of time that you spent reading:

1. Using a stopwatch, time how long it takes you to read a selected passage of material – for example, a single page within a book.
2. Calculate the average number of words per line by counting the number of words in the first three lines of the text and dividing by three (you could do this with

more sentences, but a minimum of three should yield a fairly reliable average).

3. Count the number of lines in the whole passage and multiply by the average number of words per line to give the total word count (if it's a long passage spanning multiple pages, calculate the number of words per line and lines per page to get an average word count per page).

4. Then divide this by the time in minutes it took you to read through the text. If you read three pages averaging 400 words a page in four minutes, you have a speed of 300 words per minute (3 x 400, divided by 4).

If you're regularly drilling the techniques covered here, you should soon see an increase in your reading speed. Track your improvement by setting aside a few minutes every week to test your speed.

Top tip: Apps to help you train

There are plenty of free web apps designed to help you turbocharge your reading speed. Just fire up your browser and you're ready to practice at your pace.

ZapReader.com spits out text onscreen, much like a tennis ball machine fires out balls in rapid succession. You can paste in a block of text to practice with, or the URL of a website, which ZapReader will scrape for text.

By default, it allows you to read at 300 words per minute, one word at a time. However, you can alter the settings to flash words at anywhere from 25 to 1,500 words per minute, and up to 10 words at a time.

AccelaReader.com works in much the same way. It will prompt you to paste in some text, which it will then flash onscreen.

You can control reading speed, how many words to display at a time, text size, text color, and text alignment (centered, justified, etc).

Spreeder.com is very similar to AccelaReader. Start off with some of the default introductory text, or paste in your own. Spreeder will then flash the text on the screen.

You can control reading speed, how many words to display at a time, text size, text color, and text alignment (centered, justified, etc).

Reading with purpose

There is nothing inherently wrong with reading passively. With poetry or fiction, for example, it pays to keep an open mind and allow yourself to be swept away.

When you're reading for business, study or some other equally prosaic purpose, however, it's best to go in with a plan of attack. Familiarize yourself with the basics of the text you're reading. Identify what it's likely to cover, and what kind of information you hope to extract from it. Remember: reading absolutely everything from beginning to end is overkill. Your time is better spent focusing purely on the most valuable material.

Pre-reading

Think the process of reading starts when you pick up the book? Technically, that might be the case, but it's not necessarily the most effective way to go about things. You'll be a much more efficient reader if you invest a few minutes into preparation.

Decide what it is you wish to learn from the text at hand. Knowing what you're looking for will make it easier to recognize useful information when you find it. Have you ever learned a new phrase, then started to notice it crop up everywhere? That's because once you were alerted to its existence and meaning, you became much more receptive to it. Once you've established why you're reading, and what kinds of nuggets you hope to glean from it, your brain will be primed to spot them as you read.

Successful skimming hinges on efficiency. This is much easier when you know where you can expect to find certain types of information.

No matter what you're reading, there's bound to be plenty of filler material that isn't crucial to absorb. With a little practice, you'll quickly come to learn the difference and how to instinctively separate the wheat from the chaff – the latter of which you can skim over or skip entirely.

Obviously, you'll want to zero in on the parts that are dense with information. As a rule, broader or more general information is presented at the start and end of a book, and the start and end of individual chapters and paragraphs. Specific details and examples tend to be sandwiched in the middle.

For starters, try looking over these elements before anything else:

• Table of contents – this will give you an idea as to what parts of the book pertain to the subject areas you're most interested in. Take note of how the book is divided into chapters, and within those, into sections and subsections.

• Index – this will give you an idea as to the most important and frequently used terms in the book (and where to find them).

• Introduction/preface – this offers further context for the book.

• Conclusion – this will sum up the key points made in the book.

• Any graphs, tables, or images – these are generally used to convey important information and are content-rich.

• Section or chapter headings – these will further your understanding of the book's structure and key topics.

• Bullet points, study questions or tests at the end of chapters – these often summarize the key messages in the chapter.

Skimming over this top-level organizational information will give you a handle on the bigger picture of the overall subject before you start to read in earnest. As a result, you should find it easier to understand the text.

Before embarking on a chapter, look over the pages quickly for bold or italic print, lists or numbered items, repeated words or other indicators of important information. Scan the opening and closing sentences. Topic sentences advance a thesis point in a logical manner; the other surrounding sentences expand upon the point, providing further evidence or explanations. Look for the main ideas so that you can read with these at the forefront of your mind.

Journal articles

Journal articles have a unique and fairly fixed structure.

Abstracts provide an overview of the research topic and the results.

Introductions provide context by way of previous research in the field and an outline of the aim of the study.

Method sections describe the specific methodology used in the study.

Results sections describe the findings made.

Discussion or conclusion sections interpret the results and relate them to the original hypothesis, identify any problems, discuss the implications and suggest further research to be conducted.

While every section of a journal article relates to the other sections (the aim will shape the design of the study, while the methodology used impacts on the types of results, for example), the abstract, introduction and conclusion will be the most useful as a starting point for readers looking to maximize their time. Diving further into the method and results sections can be the next step if more detail is required.

Reading

Once you know roughly what the thrust of a particular text is, you can start filling in the blanks.

From the moment you begin reading, you should be trying to answer a few questions in your mind:

Who ... are the key people involved?
What ... are the main arguments?
Why ... do they believe these to be true?
How ... do these concepts work?

One way to improve your reading speed and comprehension (which will also force you to concentrate harder) is to mentally turn chapter headings into questions, then attempt to answer these as you read. For example, if a heading reads Influenza and the Elderly, you could transform this into How Can We Reduce Influenza Deaths Among the Elderly? Scan the text for further insights and see what conclusions you can draw.

The best speed readers are constantly asking questions and generating hypotheses as they go. Never hesitate to ask 'why?' or 'how?' or to question any aspect of the material. Identify any weaknesses or gaps in evidence that could lead to a flawed conclusion. Try imagining that you are having a debate with the author.

Making predictions about upcoming information in following sections, then skimming for confirmation of your ideas, will also keep you on your toes and enhance your comprehension of the text.

Alongside this, you should be trying to draw connections between the various concepts outlined in a text, and relating this new information to what you already know. *Speed Reading* author Tony Buzan calls this the "integrative" factor – finding patterns, and putting together what you've just learned with associated knowledge already stored in your brain.

As you read, you'll start to notice what kinds of writing devices authors use over and over – extra phrases or anecdotes that don't really add much of substance to the text. Skipping over these won't greatly detract from the experience, so feel free to give them a miss.

Many factors affect how quickly you can finish a given text: familiarity with the subject, clarity of purpose (why are you reading it?) and the level of jargon (the vocabulary used can make it difficult to get through quickly).

Remember, efficient speed reading involves varying your pace as needed – speeding up over easier and straightforward material, and conversely, slowing down for denser information. Some things, like highly scientific or legal text, should be read slowly. Use your judgment; would you rather read one crucial paragraph multiple times or an entire page hammering home the same concept?

Read it three times

We previously discussed how backtracking is the enemy of speed reading. However, there is a school of thought that recommends reading material through three times, where each reading serves a different purpose.

Phase 1 is the pre-reading stage, where you simply need to get your head around the outline of the book and identify the writer's purpose and conclusions. The first time around is about whipping through the pages to get a feel for the structure and the flow of information. You might make a note of key passages that warrant a closer look when you return for a more in-depth reading.

Phase 2 involves reading to understand. Set aside more time for this stage. The goal is to gain a deeper overview of the whole picture – enough so that you can not only recount the key points, unaided, but also so that you are positioned to critically evaluate the material from an informed perspective. This is where you fill in the blanks and connect the dots.

Phase 3 entails committing the most crucial points to memory. This stage should take up more time than Phase 1 but less time than Phase 2. This time around, take notes outlining the main arguments and evidence. As you record the information by hand, you will process it mentally at the same time. If you're struggling with any concepts, this is the time to go over them again and really drill them in.

Top tip: Don't overdo it

Your mind isn't tireless, and unfortunately, your capability for retention and understanding decreases after a fairly short burst of prolonged concentration. It's better to read a book over a few shorter sessions of no longer than a couple of hours each, punctuated by frequent and regular breaks, than one long uninterrupted marathon. You might feel particularly accomplished if you can sustain that kind of pace, but overloading your brain could actually have the opposite of the desired effect.

Taking breaks will let your newly acquired knowledge soak in and give your brain time to unconsciously process the information. When you pick your book up once again, ask yourself what you recall from where you left off, and what you still have to cover. And of course, taking breaks is also important if you care about keeping your eyes healthy and reducing strain.

Pay attention to your environment as well. A quiet atmosphere, a comfortable chair, and sufficient light will all enhance your speed reading ability. Physical discomfort or distractions can quickly derail an excellent speed reading session.

Key takeaway

With a little practice, you'll quickly learn how to zero in on the best material and discard the fluff. First look at tables of contents, introductions or conclusions, chapter summaries, and headings or bolded text to see at a glance what the key points are. When reading, focus on the most valuable content, and don't be afraid to slow down if you encounter a passage that requires a little more concentration on your part to grasp.

Don't be a passive reader. Engage by constantly asking yourself questions about the material and double-checking your own assumptions, and relating new information to other knowledge you already have.

Memorization and study tips

Reciting

The next stage in the reading process is reciting. What on earth is that, you ask?

This is the first step toward ensuring that you are absorbing the material in front of you. The key elements of reading are speed, comprehension, and recall. Sometimes we must trade off comprehension for speed to a degree, but there's no point tearing through a thick textbook if you retain nothing from it.

In order to increase your reading speed, you must decide how thoroughly you need to understand the material at hand. Remember, you don't need to read every single word from beginning to end. Generally, it's more important to have a good handle on the key points than to linger over every small detail.

You should be summarizing the content frequently as you read and monitoring your comprehension. Every so often, pause to ask yourself what you've learned. After finishing a chapter or section, run over the key points in your head, and visualize them if possible. This will help you commit them to memory.

They say the best way to learn is by teaching someone else. Sharing your newly acquired knowledge with somebody else will help close the loop and cement the facts in your mind. So try telling a friend over the phone about a few of the key points you've learned, imparting a couple of ideas to your Facebook or Google Plus followers, penning a blog post, or bringing them up next time you get together with friends. Discussing what you've read will reinforce your grasp of the material. And it might even inspire others.

Another tactic to help boost your recall is making separate notes detailing what you've read. Study strategies all emphasize good note taking. Here are a few pointers.

Note taking

Have you ever gotten to the end of a page or the end of a chapter, only to realize you have no understanding or recollection of what you just read?

Welcome to note taking. Good notes will serve you well, not only because you can refer to them later, but because the very act of recording key points in writing drills them further into your brain and increases the likelihood that you will remember them unassisted.

Your notes should include the bare basics – a skeleton outline of the most important concepts, without going into extraneous detail. Your notes should be sufficient to 'jumpstart' your brain, triggering recall of further corresponding information that expands on each point.

How much information should you be jotting down? This will vary widely, but as a rule, you shouldn't average more than a couple of lines per page.

Avoid copying sentences verbatim. Rather, you should be selectively distilling them into their most basic points and using your own words. You have a much better shot at remembering information when you take the time to paraphrase it, giving it some thought and translating it into language you would use. While this does take longer than merely 'cutting and pasting', it's a good investment of your time.

In fact, there's no need to write in complete sentences at all. Symbols, abbreviations, acronyms and short phrases are your friends here. As long as your notes have meaning to you and you can decipher them later, that's the main thing.

How you choose to format your notes is up to you. It's a matter of personal preference. Some people like to highlight important points or use different colours for headings, for example. Some prefer a structured layout while others adopt a more fluid one.

There are many common note taking strategies out there. While you don't need to stick to a formal template, it can be useful to see what the experts recommend.

One of the more popular note taking methods is known as the Cornell method. When using the Cornell method, the page is essentially divided into three parts. Notes are jotted down in one, key words and concepts are recorded in another (referred to as the recall column), and a summary follows at the bottom.

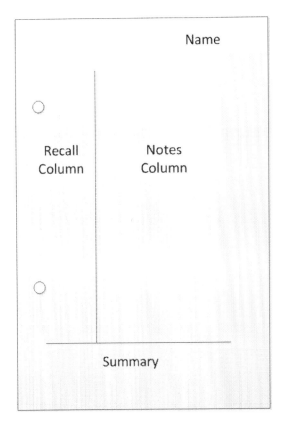

Another common note taking method is the outline format. The outlining strategy involves organizing information in order from broad to most specific, drilling down from the top. It tends to be heavy on bullet points, with supporting information for each topic threaded and indented below. It's especially useful when you are studying one topic in depth or need to organize information into logical categories.

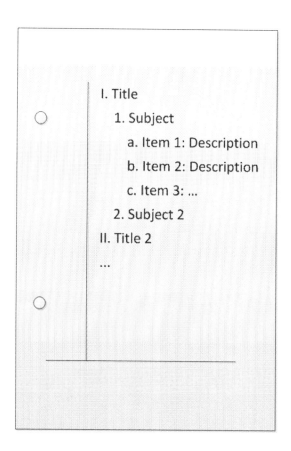

Reviewing

Reviewing is the final step, in which you organize your newly acquired knowledge and begin to build up your memory bank in earnest.

Once you've completed a text, reread your outline, and then attempt to recite it from memory. Quiz yourself on the key points, discuss them with others, and take any opportunity to further cement your understanding of the material. Reading, writing, visualizing and listening all engage different parts of the brain.

Here are a few more study tips to help you get that information to stick.

Memorization tricks

Acronyms

Using the first letter in each word from a group of words to form a new word creates an acronym. Ideally, this should be a word you are familiar with, or something unusual or catchy that's likely to stick in your head.

They're actually incredibly common in everyday life; you probably know more of them than you think. How about ASAP (as soon as possible), NASA (National Aeronautics and Space Administration) or UFO (unidentified flying object)?

If you're trying to remember a list, phrase or a string of words in a specific order, acronyms are a great way to memorize them. A couple of common educational acronyms are ROY G BIV for the colors of the rainbow (Red, Orange, Yellow, Green, Blue, Indigo, Violet) and PEMDAS for the mathematical order of operations (Parentheses, Exponents, Multiplication, Division, Addition, Subtraction).

Acronyms are useful for rote memorization, but they're not ideal for more in-depth comprehension. Also, not all lists lend themselves well to acronyms.

Acrostics

Acrostics are similar to acronyms, but instead of using the first letters of words to make a new word, you use them to create sentences. A common acrostic used to remember the order of planets in the solar system is **M**y **v**ery **e**nergetic **m**other **j**ust **s**erved **u**s **n**ine **p**izzas (Mercury, Venus, Earth, Mars, Jupiter, Saturn, Uranus, Neptune).

Essentially, you're building a sentence with the same number of words, which may seem totally counterintuitive and a waste of time, but if the resulting sentence is more memorable than the original string of words, then you're onto a winner.

Again, they're great for memorizing ordered lists, and are less limiting than acronyms – you have more freedom and flexibility. However, they can take more work to create and do require you to remember more – a sentence as opposed to one word.

Chunking

Learning to chunk is crucial to increasing your reading speed. Chunking is also a handy way of memorizing information – just in a different context.

Our short-term memory is limited, and one way to get around this is to memorize fewer, but larger, items. For example, you could try to remember the number 5359324909 – or you could break it up into chunks, e.g. 535 932 4909. That way, instead of remembering 10 individual digits, you need only remember three separate groups of numbers.

A common rule of thumb is that people can hold around seven items in their short-term memory bank. That's the logic behind phone numbers!

Making up rhymes and songs

Adding a tune into your study arsenal is another way to aid retention. One of the very first things you ever learned would have been the alphabet, taught to you using the *Twinkle, Twinkle, Little Star* melody. Repeating a familiar rhythm and melody but adding in new information is a handy memory trick that's quite effective.

Visualize mental images

Humans are visual creatures, and most of us are predominantly visual learners. That means we learn best by seeing things. By linking information to an image, you help cement that knowledge in your mind. Juxtaposing ridiculous items within the same picture can help – for example, imagining a crocodile under a McDonald's arch to remember founder Ray Krok, or an IV drip hooked up to a coconut to remember that coconut water is almost identical to blood plasma.

You can use this method in many ways. It could be as simple as visualizing a square with the letters M and C within, and the letter E outside ($E=MC2$). Or to learn a new word and its definition, try breaking it up into syllables, brainstorming words that can be associated with those syllables (for example, rhyming words) then splicing together the images for those words to make a single wacky mental picture.

Try it with a simple shopping list. You might need to buy a sponge, a broom, orange juice, vinegar, chicken, bread, ham and cheese, 8 things total. So how about you think of a live chicken, eating a ham and cheese sandwich, holding a broom that has a sponge at the top, which is soaked with an ugly combination of orange juice and vinegar. Then just remember it was 8 things (or you could think of the chicken wearing 8-shaped sunglasses) and there you have it! Wacky, but it works.

Flash cards

Making up flash cards to quiz yourself is another common study technique. Usually, you write part of a fact to prompt yourself on one side of the card, and the rest of the fact on the other side. For example, you might list the first three items in a list on one side, and try to fill in the blanks yourself. If you get stuck, you can turn the card over to see the answers.

Mind maps

We've already covered note taking, but we haven't touched on brainstorming or mind mapping. The main idea behind mind mapping is creating a comprehensive visual diagram, which is great for demonstrating the relationships between ideas or things.

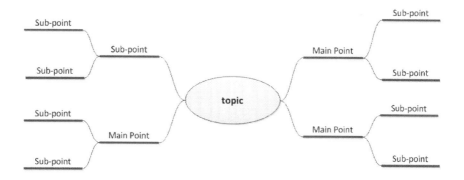

Start by identifying the most central concept, either a word or short phrase. Write this in the center of the page and circle it. Then build outwards from there, drawing branches and sub-branches to create associations between items.

31

Use key words, phrases and symbols that represent ideas and objects, rather than full-blown sentences. Think about how each piece relates to the central idea, and place closely related items nearest the middle. Where possible, try to group or cluster related ideas in the same areas of the page.

Learn by doing

Kinesthetic learning, which is also known as tactile learning, is a style of study that focuses on some type of physical activity. Learning using all your senses offers many touchpoints for reinforcing the lesson at hand. If you can see, hear, touch and even taste or smell it, you're more likely to remember it later. Muscle memory is a powerful thing (as they say, you never forget how to ride a bike).

Kinesthetic learners usually do well in activities such as science experiments, sports, art or drama. It's common for them to focus on two different tasks at once. Rather than dividing their attention unnecessarily, their retention is actually improved because they can remember something in relation to the other thing they were doing at the same time.

For example, you might choose to listen to music while reading. Many find extra noise a distraction when studying, but for some, outside stimulation actually enhances learning. If that's the case, give yourself permission to experiment: fidget, stand up or walk around while studying.

Linking words with physical gestures is another way to reinforce learning. For example, *The Learning Revolution* by Gordon Dryden and Dr Jeannette Vos outlines a particular method of learning to count in Japanese whereby each number corresponds to a matching physical action. One = ichi and two = ni, which sounds like 'itchy knee', so you would scratch your knee as you recite the words.

Finally, role play can be a valuable method of learning, depending on the subject at hand and whether you can find another person to role play with or debate with.

Make mental journeys with the Loci method

The Loci memory technique is also great for kinesthetic learners. It's sometimes referred to as the memory palace, because it involves mentally associating various pieces of information with a familiar landmark, such as rooms inside your house. Those places act as memory triggers, prompting you to recall the matching item.

Sound confusing? Here's how it works. Visualize a sequence of locations, e.g. all the rooms in your house, and the path you take to get to all of them. You might walk through the door, take off your coat in the hall, dump your keys on the kitchen counter, walk through the bedroom and then reach the bathroom. Then take a list of items that you need to learn, and mentally 'place' them in those rooms as you go. Again, exaggeration and strange juxtaposition can work in your favor here. To recall the list later on, mentally follow that same path through your house and recreate the journey, pausing in each room, at which point you will be prompted to remember the associated item.

Creativity is key here, and the possibilities are nearly endless. You could also do this with, say, the route that you take as you walk to work every day, using selected buildings, trees, sculptures, parks or other sights for landmarks.

Reading is all well and good, but in many cases it's just the beginning. To hold onto the information, you'll need to do a bit more work.

It starts with engaging with the material as you read, then mentally reviewing straight after. Note taking also helps in committing information to memory, so jotting down organized (but not painstakingly detailed) notes to refer to later is a good idea.

Beyond that, you can employ a range of study tricks to further seal your understanding. From making up simple acrostics and acronyms to comprehensive mind maps, drilling with flash cards or the Loci method, strengthening your recall is best achieved through reinforcement.

Conclusion

The world champions of speed reading can typically read between 1,000 and 2,000 words per minute. The rest of us operate at perhaps 10 percent of that.

However, using the tried and true techniques that are the cornerstone of speed reading, you can double or triple your reading rate without much effort.

By now, you should have a solid grasp on the key elements of speed reading, as well as memorization tricks and system to boost retention. As you've learned, speed reading is not a gimmick, but a proven way of absorbing and retaining knowledge more efficiently.

Given how much information we deal with on a daily basis, learning to speed read and improve your recall will help you blast through the deluge of content and become more of a power player at work or school. You now have the ability to deal with all the material that lands in your inbox, on your desk, etc.

Like any habit, you'll find your speed reading might become rusty with a lack of practice. But it's like riding a bicycle – once you nail the basics, you'll never forget. Speed reading is a skill that will serve you well throughout your life.

Make a plan today:

Commit to practicing. You might want to set aside time for this first thing in the morning, so you don't risk skipping a day because you're too tired in the evening. Just set your alarm 45 minutes earlier if you need to. Read for at least 30 minutes, being mindful of both speed and comprehension.

Do this for four weeks. It takes approximately a month to form a new habit. Once it's ingrained into your daily routine, you won't even have to think about it.

Make notes after each reading to capture what you've learned, and set aside time to review them on the weekend, or even discuss them with friends and family.

Test your reading speed regularly – once or twice a week – and monitor the changes. As you make progress, don't forget to reward yourself! And feel free to email info@readsuperfast.com to share your results!

Suggested further reading

10 Days to Faster Reading (Abby Marks-Beale)

Speed Reading in a week (Tina Konstant)

Speed Reading: Accelerate Your Speed And Understanding For Success (Tony Buzan)

Speed Reading For Professionals (H Bernard Wechsler)

The Learning Revolution (Gordon Dryden and Dr Jeannette Vos)

For future updates and more on Speed Reading, please visit
www.readsuperfast.com

If this book was useful to you, please consider
leaving a review!

Made in the USA
Lexington, KY
10 November 2014